BLOOD MEMORY

POEMS BY

Gail Newman

MARSH HAWK PRESS

2020

FIRST EDITION

1   3   5   7   9   10   8   6   4   2

Marsh Hawk Press books are published by Marsh Hawk Press, Inc.,
a not-for-profit corporation under section 501 (c)3
United States Internal Revenue Code

Library of Congress Cataloging-in-Publication Data
Newman, Gail, author.
Blood memory / Gail Newman.
First edition. | East Rockaway, New York : Marsh Hawk Press, 2020.
Summary: *Blood Memory* traces the trajectory of a family from
Poland to America during and after World War II. The themes of the poems
encompass memory, immigration, assimilation, and the legacy and impact
of genocide on the second generation. *Blood Memory* is a eulogy to the dead
and a tribute to the survivors, a book about courage and hope.
LCCN 2019036433 | ISBN 978-0-9969911-9-3 (paperback)
LCC PS3614.E6235 A6 2020 | DDC 811/.6—dc23
LC record available at https://lccn.loc.gov/2019036433
ISBN 978-0-9969911-9-3

Book design by Heather Wood
www.HeatherWoodBooks.com

Printed in the USA

Marsh Hawk Press
P.O. Box 206, East Rockaway, NY 11518-0206
www.MarshHawkPress.org

❧

for my parents

Felice Newman
Faiga Winer

Morris Newman
Moshe Israel Najman

הכרבל ונורכיז, of blessed memory

Contents

III

LIVING WITH THE DEAD

I

BLOOD MEMORY

Prayer to Remember

I came to a house where the door was ajar,
and the light of the living shone through.

I dreamt I was holy; I dreamt I was blessed.
God poured a pitcher of pity into the world.

I lay down in deep grass to find solace
beside gravesites sheltered in shadow.

The First and Last

Early in the war, when her father was taken—

before the ghetto,
before starvation and the deportations,

before Rumkowski pleaded,

> *Brothers and sisters, give them to me!*

before the children hid in basements, inside heaps
of garbage, in fields, covered with leaves
and branches, before my own father concealed himself
under a mattress, before

> *I must cut off limbs in order to save the body*—

my mother walked alone down the Jew-shuttered street
to ask the collaborator for news of the dead.

After the Hanging

Breziny, 1939

The band, some shouldering violins,
began to play.
Children, lifted up,
were cautioned not to look away.

Fajga, the water carrier, standing by the well,
raised the bucket but did not drink.
Mundzia, the mad, laughed and cried,
her sandals sinking in mud.

The soldiers ordered the women
to crouch at their feet kissing the filthy boots.
Apple trees hung in bloom, pollen vanishing
into the muddled air.

My father must have stood in that crowd,
one hand pressing his glasses
to the bridge of his nose,
the other hand fingering scraps
of fabric and tailor's chalk in his pocket.

Taken

Łódź, 1939

After her father was taken away,
and her mother's hair turned white
overnight, my mother began to grieve.
The younger brother, born sickly,
lay in bed shivering. They drank glasses
of milky tea and locked the doors. Waited.
On the streets, in fedoras and dark clothes,
Jews walked close to buildings, eyes averted.
Shops boarded shut, *Juden* posted in windows.
Yellow stars sewn onto coats. For one year
they waited, then halfway through another.
Schools closed. Friends disappeared.
Snow melted into slush. Yesterday
melted into tomorrow. Then a notice came,
and my grandmother went out into the city,
along roads where the branches of the trees
were black as ash, and came back with a package
in her arms, and she set it on the table,
opened it, and as the children watched,
lifted out a bundle of clothes—
socks, pants, blood-soaked shirt,
the smell of flesh, the empty
smoldering sleeves.

Breath

Did you ever have a family?

Yes. And a table. Chairs. My brother slept
in a bed beside my bed.

Our voices were thick with singing
as we walked the rain-stained streets—

horse-stink, cabbages, the sky camouflaged
under chimney smoke from textile factories.

Home was everywhere in that place.
And we were the stories our parents told.

Did you ever have a family?

I did. It was winter.
We skated on the drugged frost of God's breath

as if the world was a frozen lake
and we in our mittens and cloth coats

could not see the cold clouds
rising from our own mouths.

Did you ever have a family?

My father carried in his pocket,
my hand, our paces in step,

others walking toward us in black fedoras
and colored kerchiefs, a crunch

underfoot of dry leaves, snow,
apple blossoms, earth.

One was taken, then another.
The rooms of the houses shrank with loss.

Neighbors pulled shirts and socks, still damp,
in from the line. Children were kept indoors.

A woman was hauled by her hair
down a public street and no one called out.

They looked away. They said later they did not see—
in open daylight, at the news stand,

in front of the café—

My Mother in the Łódź Ghetto

Every day my mother crossed a bridge
from one world to another.
On one side, women hid apples under their coats
to throw over the wall in the dark.
On the other side, bodies littered the ground.
My mother's job was to tally the dead,
making notations—name, address, age,
body bloated or bone-thin.
Some were children. They had been pushed
to the side or into the gutter, where my mother
stepped around or over them—
their bodies cold, blue, finished
with God.

Sabotage

The Łódź Ghetto Documents Office

Her left hand on the table
holds steady an index card,
while with the right she rubs off
the damning curled leg
of a five, the ample breast of a zero,
adding a loop to make a number older,
erasing another to diminish the truth.

Though the card is unlined, the script
soldiers straight across the page.
With feet rooted on the floor,
hands soiled with lead, she bends
over the table—working
through the thin hours.

Satisfied, she settles the card
back in the box and pulls free another,
while outside, clouds race over the city,
the sky bending into tomorrow's light.

The evidence is in her hands.
A Jewish girl—my mother—
in the year of her awakening.

Transport

A train came to a stop.
The doors opened.
Those still alive stumbled out,
my mother clinging
on one side to her mother,
on the other side to her brother.
They were ordered to stand.
It was spring, April, but the air was thick
with an odor of ash and decay.
Smoke rose, blackening the sky.
Was it night or day? They did not know.
Those who trusted God began to pray.
Others left Him discarded on the tracks
as the train pulled away.

Cousins in Auschwitz

After the lines parted—
my grandmother sent to the left,
my mother and Malka sent to the right—

their heads shaven,
clothes taken away,
my mother was given shoes,

one black, one brown,
while Malka disappeared
in a dress that fell to the floor.

In the camp, my mother and Malka kept close.
They shared crumbs, stood together
at roll call. When the kapo slapped my mother
and her glasses fell to the ground,

Malka picked them up
out of the dust, settled them back
over my mother's eyes.

They kept alive,
pressed together on a wooden plank,
strangers above and below,
one's breath on the other's face.

My Mother Remembers

Hafsstadt Labor Camp

We walked, every morning, through the town,
while it was still dark—so the people could not see,
and could say later they did not know.

We were skinny, barefoot or in torn shoes,
walking on stones and in dirt to the factory
where we fit metal parts into little holes.

Piece by piece, bending our heads down to the work,
we put the wrong part in the wrong hole,
so the guns would not fire.

Then we walked back through the town,
the smell of bread and meat in the street.
After we were locked in at night,

two hundred women and girls,
the guard gone until morning, we were left
together, sitting and talking like home.

I told stories from books I had read,
Anne of Green Gables

> *If I wasn't a human girl, I think I'd like to be a bee and live among
> the flowers.*

I remembered the words,
and told the stories
until we forgot where we were,

Well, that is another hope gone.

leaning together on cots,

My life is a perfect graveyard of buried hopes.

until soldiers threw stones
at the window, yelling, *Come out.*
Come out. The war is over!

Still Life, 1945

War. The man face-down in the snow is my father.
Chest, legs, body as if asleep in snow. He hears the silent
woods, the slight shiver of ice forming on branches,
the cry of a crow, crunch of boots, artillery fire,
moans. Allied planes overhead, crush of metal, shouts.
He imagines his mother lies down beside him,
smooths his hair, breathes with him.
Something in the world must love him.
Must want him alive—his hands, the soles of his feet,
the veins in his neck, the roots of his hair.
He feigns death. For three days
unmoving in the snow, his bones
so cold they could break.

Exile

We traveled by train.
The borders were open.
We had no papers, no photographs or passports.
We were stopped. Searched. Raped.
God pushed us forward like someone shoving
at the back of a line. What were we waiting for?
Soup. Bread. We found any way home.
When we got to Łódź, the city was still standing,
the factories and shops, the windows unbroken,
the streets leading to the square.
But my mother was gone, my father, my brother.
The baker and the rabbi, the seamstress,
the cobbler, and the dog.
God said, *Go back.* God said, *Run!*

Homecoming

My mother came to a dead end called Poland.
The shops gone, the house no longer home.
She knocked at the door. A man answered.
She could see over his shoulder into the living room,
her mother's lamp, her father's chair.
She could hear music swinging from the radio,
post-war American bands. She asked to come in,
just for a minute to take a breath of the air
that might still carry her father's cigarette smoke,
the scent of her mother's soup,
the pencils she sharpened at the desk.
No. No, and again, *No.*
Words she would carry with her
wherever she went—away from Łódź,
Krakow, Bialystok, away
from the street that was not her street,
the city that was not her city,
a coat that was no longer her mother's coat—
someone else's arms in the sleeves—
a stranger who came to the door,
wearing her father's shoes.

The Dispossessed

Mother

I left my father's shoes, laces untied,
*   beside the suitcase in the hallway.*

I left my schoolbooks, my honor badge
*   and my application to University.*

I left the buildings stacked like dominoes and the statue
*   of our hero in the plaza where four streets converged.*

I left the rain staining the upstairs window
*   and the courtyard where women washed laundry in a tin tub.*

I left pigeons in the park roosting in dusty trees,
*   and the Mandelbrot in the bakery, and the braided challah.*

I left behind my name and my good young body,
*   and I went wandering,*

a refugee, my dark hair shorn
*   and a broken comb in my pocket.*

Father

I left behind my mother's shadow spilling like grain
  through the doorway of the house.

I left the smoke of my father's cold breath
  and the horses inside the shed.

I left the lake, a wooden boat, girls'
  fingers dangling in the eddies.

I left the lark, the cherry tree,
  and the bundled lilacs dripping from branches.

I left my sewing needles and thread, and woolen cloth
  cut in patterns on the table.

I left behind my name and the work of my hands,
  and I went wandering,

a refugee with holes in my pockets
  and cardboard in my shoes.

This Hallway Called Earth

Near the platform, stacks of valises stamped with home addresses,
jumbled piles of clothes, heaped shoes, gold teeth, jewels and gold
coins.

*Don't worry, my friend, don't worry, my friend, just
don't worry.*

They asked permission to say a prayer for the dead.

You, tall dog, come over here.

In summer, the town stood window high in wild flowers.

The children were so hungry, they could neither hear or see.

Words became muffled distant sounds.

Small puddles of water in a potato field.
Down the endless white-shrouded roads.

*The forest is filthy with Jewish blood.
You will lick it with your tongues until it is spotlessly clean.*

※※※

When they place my transgressions on one side of the scale,
on the other side, I will place my concentration camp uniform.

For there is nothing more wholesome than a broken Jewish heart.

※※※

A ladle full of soup.

Passover came and went.

Mushrooms and berries in the forest. Leather truncheons, disinfectant, broken clogs.

He spat on his cousin's forehead, pressed his own forehead against his cousin's. Led him by the hand to the group marked with stars.

Some Godly sparks left in men and some humanity in God.

※ ※ ※

I was walking toward my mother's voice.

Heads shaven, dressed in gray, with wooden clogs on swollen feet, six abreast, we marched through the main gate.

We walked through snow-covered fields and frozen roads, through villages where blue smoke rose from chimneys. We begged for bread, but no one heard us.

Then it was springtime and lilac bushes were in full bloom.

My mother's voice was very near.

II

LOST LANGUAGE

I Came into the World

My father was there, my mother.
I came into a room where the table was laid
as if for a banquet, figs on white plates,
cool water. Like a stranger, I stood aside, hesitant.
Music rose up and pushed against the ceiling,
shimmered there like a crystal chandelier.
People were singing. The floor shook with dance.
I came into a house where I was a stranger
and was made welcome.
My mother gave me her body, my father
his voice. I stood between them, faltering.
The walls of the house rose up around us.
The roof shuddered with the sound of wind and rain.
Birds settled in the rafters. At night we could hear them,
the shuffling of feathers, melodies marking territory,
saying, *This is mine; this is real.*

A Short Engagement

Landsberg, Displaced Persons' Camp, 1945

They were walking at night
along the river, because, my father
said, *It was romantic,*
and everything after the war
was beautiful. This was not home,
but it was somewhere.

But because it was after curfew—the bridge
dark over the water, shades
pulled across the windows—
they were arrested.

Can you believe it? After Auschwitz.
Kelevs! Ganifs!

Three months later my parents were married.
We had a cow, but we had to wait
until we found a shochert.

We were young people. It was a pleasure, living
like a family. Food out of this world,
my mother said.
A potato. A shtik broyt.

Everything

My father brings home a dog
who guards me in my cradle,
growling at my mother
when she steps close.
My aunt is in the house, baking.
She sets a broken pan under the stove
for safe-keeping.
My mother has gone off to work—
I don't know who she is,
mistaking my father's sister
for the one who loves me best.
I cry and cry until the doctor says
to my mother, *You don't have enough milk.*
My mother looks down at her breasts,
small as apples. It is too soon after the war,
and my parents want so much right away.
Everything they own is in my body.

Lost Language

I walk along a road pronouncing
words: *winter, field, landscape, obscure.*

In the distance a field appears,
an obscure landscape, trees weeping white

frost from childhood, not the country I grew up in
but the one where I was born,

where my father traded coffee for bread
and rocked me in a cradle, a string tied

to his big toe while he slept beside my mother,
snow forming crystal angels on the windows.

I mumble random words, alphabets of a lost
tongue, alert for the perfect lexicon,

the one that will free me from longing
and loneliness: *zayde, earth, l'chaim, faith.*

Mameloshen, words of endearment, words that women
spoke in the street, bargaining for carp, bagging radishes,

How much, *Vi ful?* Greeting a neighbor, *Guten tak,*

while the men intoned holy words to each other
in the temple pews and on the bima—

Shepsele, Ketsele, Shaya Punim, Meyn Kinde—

How I love you more than life.

Tsebrokhn English

Gai avek. Gai gezunterhait! they said. *Gai in drerd arein!*
My father's lexicon, *Gai kuken ahfen yam!* So, we went
away in health to hell. Shitting in the ocean.

My mother who never swore said only, *Gai shoyn, gai,*
or *Genug iz genug!* Go already! Enough is enough!

Speak English! I'd plead at Orbach's, fondling pleated skirts,
or just walking down the street past windows
full of used refrigerators and fake crystal bowls, past beauty salons
and liquor stores and bakeries with rye bread behind glass.

Gai platz, the uncles would shout in unison, no one
listening. *Gai mit dein kop in drerd.*
Summer nights or in the kitchen when the kinder were pretending
sleep, they'd murmur, *Gedainst?* Remember?

and their voices would take on a tone
like burnt toast or trampled flowers, an ache we never heard
in daylight. And the English would fade away like smoke
until only the Yiddish remained, and we were foreigners
in our own houses, with strangers for parents.

Mishpacha

My aunt kept a strap hanging on the wall,
though my cousins, years later, swore
she never used it.

My uncle stood outside the kitchen window,
barefoot in the dark, outstretched hands
inside his shoes, mumbling;

Fres, Fres Kindele. Eat. Eat.
or Baba Yaga will get you—

that old crone with the crooked grin
who sleeps naked in a house made of twigs.

I'll call the police, my mother would warn,
whipping the receiver off its cradle.

This was America, but what did we know,
green as we were, new shoots rising
from Old Country mud.

I could eat you up, the aunts chuckled, pinching
our cheeks, looming above us like cartoon
characters, words shape-shifting in the air

and we pictured them, mouths bulging
with flesh, spitting out our bones
sopping up bloody scraps on the plate,

as we tilted our heads, listening
for the truth, some great love buried
behind the threats.

Dollhouse

My father comes home with a cardboard box under his arm,
that he knifes open, removing metal walls

with tabs that bend into slits, until a house
sits, complete with flower boxes,

painted petunias, a red door, a chimney
and a warren of rooms, two stories,

with diminutive furniture, thumb-nail pans on a stove,
patches of fabric rugs and a real plastic family of four,

Americans, the father in a grey suit, blond children,
the mother with an apron tied around her waist.

And a new Buick in the garage, garden tools
lined up against the wall, a lawn mower and a drill.

That was the year my mother went away to live
for months in a hospital where I could not go.

I knew where she was
and that she would come back,

but the house seemed scraped hollow,
and in the silence, I felt someone listening,

who I thought might be God or a fairy small as a pin,
moth-like, flinging her body at the window glass.

Laundry, 1952

My mother is hanging laundry on the line.
As usual, it's summer in my memory,
the light tender and trembling.
She snaps wooden clothespins onto cotton slips,
shirts, white socks, balancing the pins in her mouth.
From the upstairs window, I watch her move
around the yard in a flowered house dress
that ties in back like an apron.
Behind her the insect drone of freeway traffic,
and beyond the alley heading west
lies the ocean, white shoulders
of sand, palm trees and the green horizon.
As she works, stringing up long sheets and pillow cases,
she lifts her arms and looks toward the window
where I watch, but she can't see me as I pull back
behind the venetian blinds. I can see the part in her hair,
her pale calves and low-heeled shoes,
eyes squinting through thick glasses.
All year I have been watching her like this,
a voyeur looking out of a window
as if there were something in that body
I could for a short time, borrow or store away
as reference for a later date.

Night Terror

1.

I've never killed anyone
or held a weapon,
yet sometimes I hear
in my head
the blast of gunfire.

My mother opens a drawer
and takes out a small blue box—

my father's wedding ring,
a broad gold band,

but where are the hands, the knuckles
and knobby wrists, the torso, the long toes?

Where is my father's chest?
Where is his heart?

2.

Some nights I wake to hear
my father crying out like a child—

night terrors—
then his slippers
brushing the floor
down the long hall,
walking past my room,
out of the apartment
into darkness that pools
around his feet like a river.

For hours, he sits
under the silence of the stars.

Then he comes back
into the house—

the clean table
covered with a yellow cloth,

the light of the moon shining through
the kitchen window
onto the red eyes of the clock.

Hunger

Some days at the table,
my father's hand is slow
to bring bread to his mouth.
He is inside the telling of his story,
his body far away, hidden under a mattress,
jumping off a train into snow,
hiding potatoes in his pockets.
We dug a trench. Then we filled it up.
Every day. Marching there and back
until it was dark. We ate cold soup,
not soup, water. Nothing.
The fork pushes food around
the plate while my father swallows
the hard words. The eggs cool.
The tea turns tepid, milk pooling
at the bottom of the cup.

Migraine

My mother goes to bed
with *a headache*, she says.
When I come from school
I know not to open her door.

My father brings home sandwiches,
the smell of newspaper on his hands.
We eat Campbell's chicken noodle soup.
Lamp light pools on the floor,

but does not pass from one room
into the dim interior of the other
where my mother lies
but does not sleep.

Later, after homework, after milk
and stories, my mother steps out
in a blue robe zipped from neck to knee,
without her glasses,

into the light of the hall, on her face
the look of an animal just out of hibernation,
washed free of memory,
winter on her skin.

Braiding

A mother, braiding, says, *Be still.*
Says, *Here is bread. Eat.*
You are tired. Rest. Take this umbrella.
Outside it is raining.

The mother closes, at night, the door.
She rolls down her stockings, unsnaps
the brassiere. Turns down her side of the bed.
The father, already asleep, does not wake.

Outside, the moon is full, spilling
as if from a bucket of warm milk
its luminous light through the window
of the room where the child sleeps,

dreaming of the blue mist above the ocean
and the blue velvet dress her father stitched
on a treadled Singer, stepping
his foot down on the pedal,

guiding the fabric between his hands,
the needle dipping in and out like a bee
inside the honey of a flower.

Come

Come as you are, bare-handed, stumbling.
Come like wild geese migrating in winter.
Come in freight cars and in cargo ships. Landlocked. Alone.
Come lonely. Come with courage and pluck.
Come with luck. Come fleeing toward freedom.
With hope. Come broke. Broken.
Come with feather pillows in your arms. Weathered. Weary.
Come with memories, knots of longing,
scarred and sore, battered, bedraggled, bewildered.
Come with your language and your candlesticks.
Come as a testament with the honey of praise
and prayer in your mouth.

III

LIVING WITH THE DEAD

Abandoned Cemeteries

Who is the trustee of the dead?
Headstones fallen over, cracked,
covered in lichen, moss, neglect.
No stones or bouquets left in remembrance.
No mourners or words of comfort.
Only the shipwrecked listen,
only the forgotten remember.

Mensch

At dinner, the two of them
are dogs, gripping chicken bones
in their teeth.

The grandfather prowls around
growling at his grandson's knees,
pretending to be smaller than he is.

Let him be a mensch, he says
at the boy's Bar Mitzvah, and when I ask
if he remembers his own, says,

No, but I remember my Bris. My father,
the family *tummler*, always with a joke,
who scrubbed the deck on a freighter to America,

while my mother and I lay below
with our eyes closed
against the tilting walls,

who landed with tuberculosis in his body
and a jacket too big for his frame,
the sting of salt in his mouth.

Two Tales

For My Father

1.

They took your clothes.
They gave you striped pajamas
in which your body swam
like someone far from shore.
They brought you to a barracks
and ordered you lie
beside others also without names.
In the morning, they marched
you to work.
In your hands, they put a shovel,
ordered you to dig. Which you did,
until the hole could swallow the sky,
big enough for you to lie down
and be done. *Fill it up*, they said.
And you did. And when it was
full they said, *Dig*, and you did.

2.

They took your clothes.
They put you in a blue gown
tied at the neck like a child's bib.
They fed you, first with a spoon,
later through a tube.
Beside the bed you heard a voice
calling your name: *Morris, Morris,*
persistent as rain on a roof.
In the hallway shoes clattered
like horses restless in stalls,
and you were walking in the woods,
frost stenciled on the trees,
breath rasping like wind
in your throat.
Then you were home inside
your mother's arms, your face
close to her breast and you
were a boy again, laughing,
with cherries staining your mouth.

The Journey

My father does not come
to me in dreams, though I wait,
patient as a monk, bags packed
to join him on his journey.

He is so deeply asleep that even the angels
cannot wake him, though they might blow
onto his face, fly with wings spread like sieves
for the light of the world to pass through,
pluck at his body, worrying his soul.

I will never see my father again.
Still, sometimes I feel him beside me,
sharpening tools, salting potatoes, breathing.

When I open my mouth his words fly out,
when I open my eyes, his tears.

Elegy

We still talk about my father
in an ordinary way.

Dad, we say, would love that flower,
or that joke, or the tie in the window

of the department store, or the collie
tethered to a parking meter.

His shoes are still in his closet,
lined up like sentries to guard the past.

The drawers, though, are empty,
no shaving cream or socks.

The last rusty bolts and lamp fixtures
are gone from the shelf in his garage.

They live in my garage now.
Someday, I will throw them away,

maybe next winter when the first storm
pours solace into the world.

Mount Sinai Jewish Cemetery

Walking on the footpath
beside the newly dead,
beneath sheltering
shadows of great oaks,
sorrow settles in my chest.

Come closer, gesture the trees,
with shuddering shoulders,
billows of wind buried
in their leaves.

I have come to the Jewish cemetery,
to talk about death.
Cremation or burial? the advance planner
asks, sliding the brochure across the desk.

I'll take the good earth, a simple pine box,
dressed in white, barefoot, face scrubbed,
my blood intact in my veins—as I am.

When I die, I won't go up in smoke,
fallen ash, with the smell of gas
in my nostrils, the fire burning
in my lungs.

If the Messiah comes,
my spine will be whole,
my leg bones fastened, so I
can stand and walk with the ashes

of my grandmother in my arms, gathered
from the forest outside Auschwitz, fallen
beside the birch trees and on the brittle
branches of the oaks and in the cracks
where beetles burrow,

and we will go together,
not led like harnessed horses
or leashed dogs

but streaming forward like the sun
when it settles on the fields in summer.

The Bridge

Inside my mother's mouth,

a gap where she's removed the bridge,
the gums darker at the base.

The bridge, sunken to the bottom
of a water-filled glass, seems

out of place, like a fish plucked
from the sea plunked into a pail.

Looking in the mirror, my mother
opens wide, pulling coated floss down

between those teeth still intact.
I didn't know you had a bridge, I say,

and she looks at me slant-wise,
as if to say, *Don't ask,*

because the world is a dark throat,
and some words are best swallowed.

In Hafsstadt my mother sat in a chair,
head back, a woman in a white coat

arched over her, pliers in hand,
the shining metal inside my mother's mouth,

wrenching left and right, the twisted teeth
loosening, my mother's arms tied down.

But I was lucky. Because she liked me,
she didn't pull the ones in front,

my mother says,
white teeth gleaming

behind a narrow smile.

Valentine's Day

Now that my father is gone,
I send my mother flowers.

She sleeps under a blue blanket
alone on her side of the bed,
fluffing both pillows just so.

She balances as she walks,
one hand skimming the wall.
Sometimes she doesn't know
where her friends are, who is still living.

Einstein was right about time
moving in two directions at once,
how everything that happens
seems to have happened before,

how when I stand before the mirror
combing my hair, I see my mother's eyes,
and happiness wells up like a wave
without warning.

My mother looks forward
to a lunch of bread and cheese,
a glass of apple juice.

She speaks of the weather,
today being only itself.
Her time is reeling in, a line cast
from shore. But how she loves
the sea, the horizon, the flaming sun!

My mother, who knows the brutal world,
who survived while others did not,
says, *Me? I had it easy.*

Stroke

For My Mother

You are lifting a book from the table.

Then you're on the floor folded over,
head fallen to the side.

You pull down the hem of your nightgown
with the hand that still moves.

Your words dissolve in your mouth,
which is twisted to the side.

You are lying in your daughter's arms.
You know she is your daughter. You hear the echo of her voice

like the wind outside in the trees,
and the indecipherable language of birds.

The light of the television falls across the carpet
like a beacon from a galaxy beyond ours

where planets are forming, stars glowing in a radiance
that is like the love on this earth.

After the Stroke

When she takes out the bridge,
exposing gaps at the gums,

my mother suddenly is not my mother
of only minutes ago,

done up in an angora crewneck,
fresh water pearls at the throat.

She leans over the sink,
holding onto the ledge, breasts

hidden under a white towel
as I submerge a washcloth

into hot water and glide
a bar of ivory soap across her back.

In the mirror two women
move slowly, one behind the other,

both bodies grown into abundance,
heavy with years.

I count them: 96, 60, 45, 20,
until we are both girls again, big-eyed,

bows in our hair. My mother takes
off her glasses, so her face is a soft blur,

our hands now side-by-side,
mine dry, mottled as a leaf,

hers like paper, transparent.
Who can say which is the elder?

It's quiet in the bathroom, splash
of water on porcelain bowl.

March of the Living

Birkinow-Aushwitz, 2016

We rode the bus from Warsaw
past cherry trees in blossom, clouds of magnolia
clustered in loose bundles,
oak forests, linden and ancient ash,
and dachas with faded wooden flanks.

We got out of the bus.
We sat in the grass by the metal gates.
We walked the iron tracks,
set wooden plaques bearing the names
of the dead between the ribs
of the splintered rails.

We pushed our hands deep
into jacket pockets, pulled hoods
up against the rain, our shoes
covered with mud. Some wore tallit
and blue emblems on breasts.

We hovered together
on metal chairs set up before
the stage. Songs were sung.
Banners raised along with umbrellas.
A survivor came on to the stage,
clinging to his granddaughter's arm.
Dressed in the uniform of death,
striped pajamas and a cap,
his voice lifted up to the crowd.

He spoke so long, they tried to lead him
from the stage, with apology at first,
them firmly, but he fought them.
He stood his ground, growing taller
with resistance,
throwing words into the rain,
his voice like the darkness inside a tunnel.

He fought until they began to sing *Yiddishe Mame.*
How dark it is when God takes her away.

He stood at attention listening
to a far-away sound
the rest of us could not hear.

Lost

I lost my wedding ring in Auschwitz,
in the dust of the railroad tracks,
a diamond set like an eye
in the blood-nourished earth.

The ring is buried among dead
leaves and the footprints of the living
who wander the barracks,
chattering to quell the silence in the walls.

The ghost of my grandmother will stoop,
back bent like a branch
in the wind, and cup the diamond
 in her hand, like a fish drawn from water,
still wet, the scent of my hands
dim on the shimmering gold.

Living With the Dead

The dead follow me around—
elbows on my shoulders
fingers in my hair,
grasping my ears.
Some days they ride me hard,
heels digging into my ribcage.
Dead, I plead, *get off my back.*
Soon I grow stupid as celery,
numb as bread. I can't feed them.
I can't wash their faces or suture
their wounds with needles of pity.
Now they are wearing my clothes,
settling blouses over their heads,
slipping pale feet into my shoes,
adjusting collars, dressed
to drape the mirrors with sheets
and stand in line to shovel dirt
into my grave.

The Field

My grandfather waits in a field of the dead.
He's given up his buttons and his flesh,
the wounds and the scars, the bruises
and abrasions. When he died, were bullets fired?
Burns inflicted? Bones broken?

He's given up his memories and his soul,
which floats above the world like cool mist.

The field in summer fills up with flowers,
capes of yellow over low grass.

I will walk there, some day, beside his grave.
I will press my lips to the earth
and whisper his name.

Blood Memory

1.

Dimitri watched from a tree. *When a woman with a baby*
approached the pit, they forced her to hold the baby in sight.
First they shot the baby and then her.

Anna remembers. *When the pit was full they filled it with a little earth.*
For three days the ground moved. Some were still alive.

Anatoly speaks the names—*Yankel, Rachel*—as if
he has been waiting all his life to say them.

The dead are patient. One century bleeds into another.
No one comes. The land stands as before,
barren of buildings, trees slouching in rain.

Snow falls.

The earth turns over, groaning in sleep.
Bodies' bones fallen one on another,
metatarsals, slender ribs, skulls leaning together,
the dead shielding the dead.

The living go on living—washing hands,
peeling apples, stirring soup, brushing hair,
tying shoe laces and sending children off to school.

They live with glass in their mouths.

2.

Last night I dreamt in Yiddish.
The dead stood behind me,
tilting like stalks of wheat.

I recognized the faces: Zeyde, Bubbe, Esther, Wolf.
I saw my father driving a horse through snow,
frost on his ears, hands ungloved.

Then he was in the fields, shaking apples from a tree,
his friends behind him, sharp-elbowed,
fuzz-cheeked, rough voices calling, *Moshe.*

I stood at the gravesites, feet soaked in mugged earth.
I lay down my body in wet leaves.
I remembered them.

Notes

Part I

"The First and Last"

> The italicized quotes are from a speech by Chaim Rumkowski who was appointed by the Nazis as head of the Jewish Council of Elders in the Łódź Ghetto. He is remembered for his speech "Give Me Your Children" in which he demanded the deportation of 20,000 children to the Chelmo extermination camp.

"After the Hanging"

> This incident was recorded in *Brzeziny Yizkor Book* (1961), published by JewishGen, Inc. and edited by A. Alperin and N. Summer.

> "Did you ever have a family?" is a line from the poem "Song and Dance" (2002) by Alan Shapiro.

"Sabotage"

> One of the most tragic events in the history of the Łódź Ghetto were the deportations from the Łódź Ghetto, when the children under ten and the elderly over sixty-five were selected for "resettlement," a Nazi euphemism for deportation to concentration camps.
>   Before the deportation, workers in the document office attempted to save lives by altering the ages of the residents.

"This Hallway Called Earth"

> In addition to the lines italicized in the poem, the following lines, as well as the title of the poem, are quotes from survivor interviews in *Hasidic Tales of the Holocaust* (1982), edited by Yaffa Eliach, Oxford University Press:

In summer, the town stood window high in wild flowers.

The children were so hungry, they could neither hear or see.

For there is nothing more wholesome than a broken Jewish heart.

Passover came and went.

Led him by the hand to the group marked with stars.

Some Godly sparks left in men and some humanity in God.

Part II

"A Short Engagement"

kelev!: male dog (derogatory word)

ganifs!: thieves (crooks)

shochert: ritual butcher

shtik broyt: piece of bread

"Lost Language"

zeyde: grandfather

l'chaim: a Hebrew toast meaning "to life"

mameloshen: Yiddish, the Jewish mother tongue

bimah: the podium or platform in a synagogue from which the
   Torah is read

shepsele: little lamb; sweetie

ketsele: little kitten

shayna punim: beautiful face

meyn kinder: my children

"Tsebrokhn English"

tsebrokhn: broken

Gai platz: Go split your guts.

Gai mit dein kop in drerd: Go stick your head in the ground.
   (Get lost.)

"Mishpacha"

Mishpacha: a Hebrew word meaning family

Part III

"Mensch"

> *mensch*: a person of integrity and honor.
>
> *bris*: the Jewish ceremony of circumcision, performed on the eighth day of the infant's life.
>
> *tummler*: an entertainer or social director; a person who makes things happen.

"Blood Memory"

> Father Patrick Desbois, a French Catholic priest, has been tracking down Nazi mass grave sites and interviewing witnesses who were children at the time of the murders. They have led him to more than 1,700 previously unknown execution sites. Italicized lines in the poem, with minor changes, are quotes from "The Hidden Holocaust," CBS, *60 Minutes* (2015).

Praise for BLOOD MEMORY

Gail Newman's *Blood Memory* speaks with an unerring directness of the Jewish experience of the Holocaust, its spare language at times reminiscent of Charles Reznikoff's chronicles of what befell the Jews of Europe in the Nazi era. But as a member of a family of survivors, her poetry, also more personal and interior, is a kind of Ark, crowded with the past but also grasping at the survivor's wish, as she sees in her mother, to be "washed free of memory." This is a painful courageous book for both reader and author. "Come with your language and candlesticks," she says, challenging that terrible history with implicit hope and confidence in her craft and imagination. "Come as testament," she insists, seeking to transform the unbearable, "with the honey of praise and prayer in your mouth."

—MICHAEL HELLER

There isn't a weak poem in the book. Writing about the Holocaust can be difficult now, not that it was ever easy. It has become myth or something people use as a metaphor for something they object to; those who know, who went through it, are dying off. Those who deny what happened multiply. To make fresh powerful poems rooted in Shoah is amazing. She does it by specifics. There are no faceless men in dirty ragged striped uniforms. The people are individualized. I found the work well-crafted, strong and moving. The structure worked well and the little poems prefacing each section was a nice touch. Her choice of details is good. The images are striking and precise. She successfully by empathy combined with research managed to enter her characters and their experiences and thus recreate them vividly.

—MARGE PIERCY

The very unspeakability of the Holocaust can make writing about it fraught. Gail Newman, the child of Holocaust survivors, transcends this difficulty in her vital new collection, *Blood Memory*, by telling her parents' stories—the story of millions—in tender, particular detail. In "The Dispossessed," we hear their voices, a lamentation of losses. Her mother: "I left behind my name and my good young body, and I went wandering, a refugee, my dark hair shorn and a broken comb in my pocket." Her father: "I left the lark, the cherry tree, and the bundled lilacs dripping from branches." Elsewhere, Newman weaves in quotes from other survivors: "Some Godly sparks left in men and some humanity in God." This is a book about collective memory, about the importance of story. Among the girls and women of the Hafsstadt Labor Camp, her mother "told stories from books I had read, *Anne of Green Gables* . . . I remembered the words, and told the stories until we forgot where we were." Newman doesn't flinch from brutality, from "the bodies, cold, blue, finished with God." Yet Newman has achieved something extraordinary. *Blood Memory* is a testament to humanity. Despite the darkness, the light of the living shines through.

—ELLEN BASS

✳✳✳

Evocative Holocaust-related poetry in this slender, though weighty, book tells much we ought never forget less all of worth also be forgotten. Terse poetic accounts of barbarous inhumanity stir anguish, grief, rage, and tears. However, other poems salute high-risk camaraderie, war production sabotage, and extraordinary life-saving resilience in ghettos, camps, and post-liberation years. Throughout, love mixes with lunacy, tenderness with torment, optimism with despair, and solace with savagery. All of us—Jewish and Gentile alike—are in the poet's debt as her art propels us forward: Would that our future never again gives cause for such a moving and unforgettable commemoration.

— ARTHUR B. SHOSTAK, SOCIOLOGY PROFESSOR
AND AUTHOR OF *STEALTH ALTRUISM: FORBIDDEN
JEWISH RESISTANCE IN THE HOLOCAUST*

Acknowledgments

Heartfelt gratitude to Ellen Bass for her support, generosity, advice, and good humor and for welcoming me into her home and poetry workshop.

Thanks to Cecilia Woloch and Kwame Dawes for assistance with the manuscript.

To Fred Marchant and The Colrain Poetry Manuscript Conference.

To Marie Howe; Martha Collins and the Fine Arts Work Center; and Maxine Hong Kingston and the Veterans Writing Group.

I am grateful to Jakub Rympel, the Polish research expert who accompanied me on a pilgrimage to find what I could of my family. Thanks to The International March of the Living: Tali Nates, Director of The Johanesburg Holocaust Museum and Jacob Shoshan.

I would like to thank Marsh Hawk Press Publisher, Sandy McIntosh, Editor, Eileen R. Tabios, and book designer Heather Wood. And to Marge Piercy—I am honored and blessed to be chosen.

All my love, gratitude, and heart to my husband, Herb Felsenfeld, and to my son, Nathan Felsenfeld, the best men I know.

Grateful acknowledgment is made to the editors of the following publications in which these poems or earlier versions of them previously appeared:

Bellingham Review, 49th Parallel Poetry Contest Award, First Prize: "Mishpacha"

The Doll Collection, Terrapin Press: "Dollhouse"

The Fourth River, Issue 15: "Exile"

Hiram Poetry Review, Issue No. 79: "The Bridge"

Jewish Journal of Northern California: "Come," "My Mother Remembers"

Mom Egg Review, Vol. 16: "Braiding"

Naugatuck River Review, Contest Issue 19: "Homecoming,"

Nimrod International Journal, Awards 41, Vol. 63 No 1: "Blood Memory"

Passager, 2018 Poetry Contest: "After the Stroke," "Sabotage," "Two Tales," "Valentine's Day"

PoetryMagazine.com, Vol. XI: "Laundry," "The Dispossessed," "I Came into the World," "Breath"

Prairie Schooner, Volume 90, Number 3: "Still Life, 1945," "Hunger" Volume 93.4: "Living With the Dead"

Prism, Volume 9: "Taken"

The Sand Hill Review, Volume XVI: "Abandoned Cemeteries"

About the Author

GAIL NEWMAN has worked as an arts administrator, museum educator at the Contemporary Jewish Museum, and CalPoets poet-teacher and San Francisco Coordinator. She was co-founder of *Room, A Women's Literary Journal* and has edited two books of children's poetry: *C is for California* and *Dear Earth*. A collection of her poetry, *One World*, was published by Moon Tide Press.

A child of Polish Holocaust survivors, Gail was born in a Displaced Persons' Camp in Lansberg, Germany, and immigrated to the United States with her family where they settled in Los Angeles. She lives in San Francisco with her husband.

TITLES FROM MARSH HAWK PRESS

Jane Augustine *Arbor Vitae; Krazy; Night Lights; A Woman's Guide to Mountain Climbing*

Tom Beckett *Dipstick (Diptych)*

Sigman Byrd *Under the Wanderer's Star*

Patricia Carlin *Original Green; Quantum Jitters; Second Nature*

Claudia Carlson *The Elephant House; My Chocolate Sarcophagus; Pocket Park*

Meredith Cole *Miniatures*

Jon Curley *Hybrid Moments; Scorch Marks*

Neil de la Flor *Almost Dorothy; An Elephant's Memory of Blizzards*

Chard deNiord *Sharp Golden Thorn*

Sharon Dolin *Serious Pink*

Steve Fellner *Blind Date with Cavafy; The Weary World Rejoices*

Thomas Fink *Selected Poems & Poetic Series; Joyride; Peace Conference; Clarity and Other Poems; After Taxes; Gossip*

Thomas Fink and Maya D. Mason *A Pageant for Every Addiction*

Norman Finkelstein *Inside the Ghost Factory; Passing Over*

Edward Foster *The Beginning of Sorrows; Dire Straits; Mahrem: Things Men Should Do for Men; Sewing the Wind; What He Ought to Know*

Paolo Javier *The Feeling is Actual*

Burt Kimmelman *Abandoned Angel; Somehow*

Burt Kimmelman and Fred Caruso *The Pond at Cape May Point*

Basil King *77 Beasts; Disparate Beasts; Mirage; The Spoken Word / The Painted Hand from Learning to Draw / A History*

Martha King *Imperfect Fit*

Phillip Lopate *At the End of the Day: Selected Poems and An Introductory Essay*

Mary Mackey *Breaking the Fever; The Jaguars That Prowl Our Dreams; Sugar Zone; Travelers With No Ticket Home*

Jason McCall *Dear Hero,*

Sandy McIntosh *The After-Death History of My Mother; Between Earth and Sky; Cemetery Chess; Ernesta, in the Style of the Flamenco; Forty-Nine Guaranteed Ways to Escape Death; A Hole In the Ocean; Lesser Lights; Obsessional*

Stephen Paul Miller *Any Lie You Tell Will Be the Truth; The Bee Flies in May; Fort Dad; Skinny Eighth Avenue; There's Only One God and You're Not It*

Daniel Morris *Blue Poles; Bryce Passage; Hit Play; If Not for the Courage*

Geoffrey O'Brien *The Blue Hill*

Sharon Olinka *The Good City*

Christina Olivares *No Map of the Earth Includes Stars*

Justin Petropoulos *Eminent Domain*

Paul Pines *Charlotte Songs; Divine Madness; Gathering Sparks; Last Call at the Tin Palace*

Jacquelyn Pope *Watermark*

George Quasha *Things Done for Themselves*

Karin Randolph *Either She Was*

Rochelle Ratner *Balancing Acts; Ben Casey Days; House and Home*

Michael Rerick *In Ways Impossible to Fold*

Corrine Robins *Facing It; One Thousand Years; Today's Menu*

Eileen R. Tabios *The Connoisseur of Alleys; I Take Thee, English, for My Beloved; The In(ter)vention of the Hay(na)ku; The Light Sang as It Left Your Eyes; Reproductions of the Empty Flagpole; Sun Stigmata; The Thorn Rosary*

Eileen R. Tabios and j/j hastain *The Relational Elations of Orphaned Algebra*

Susan Terris *Familiar Tense; Ghost of Yesterday; Natural Defenses*

Lynne Thompson *Fretwork*

Madeline Tiger *Birds of Sorrow and Joy*

Tana Jean Welch *Latest Volcano*

Harriet Zinnes *Drawing on the Wall; Light Light or the Curvature of the Earth; New and Selected Poems; Weather is Whether; Whither Nonstopping*

YEAR	AUTHOR	MHP POETRY PRIZE TITLE	JUDGE
2004	Jacquelyn Pope	*Watermark*	Marie Ponsot
2005	Sigman Byrd	*Under the Wanderer's Star*	Gerald Stern
2006	Steve Fellner	*Blind Date with Cavafy*	Denise Duhamel
2007	Karin Randolph	*Either She Was*	David Shapiro
2008	Michael Rerick	*In Ways Impossible to Fold*	Thylias Moss
2009	Neil de la Flor	*Almost Dorothy*	Forrest Gander
2010	Justin Petropoulos	*Eminent Domain*	Anne Waldman
2011	Meredith Cole	*Miniatures*	Alicia Ostriker
2012	Jason McCall	*Dear Hero,*	Cornelius Eady
2013	Tom Beckett	*Dipstick (Diptych)*	Charles Bernstein
2014	Christina Olivares	*No Map of the Earth Includes Stars*	Brenda Hillman
2015	Tana Jean Welch	*Latest Volcano*	Stephanie Strickland
2016	Robert Gibb	*After*	Mark Doty
2017	Geoffrey O'Brien	*The Blue Hill*	Meena Alexander
2018	Lynne Thompson	*Fretwork*	Jane Hirshfield
2019	Gail Newman	*Blood Memory*	Marge Piercy

ARTISTIC ADVISORY BOARD

For more information, please go to: **www.marshhawkpress.org**